Reading STREET

Program Authors

Peter Afflerbach

Camille Blachowicz

Candy Dawson Boyd

Elena Izquierdo

Connie Juel

Edward Kame'enui

Donald Leu

Jeanne R. Paratore

P. David Pearson

Sam Sebesta

Deborah Simmons

Alfred Tatum

Sharon Vaughn

Susan Watts Taffe

Karen Kring Wixson

PEARSON

Glenview, Illinois • Boston, Massachusetts • Chandler, Arizona • Upper Saddle River, New Jersey

We dedicate Reading Street to
Peter Jovanovich.

~

His wisdom, courage,
and passion for education
are an inspiration to us all.

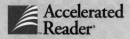

About the Cover Artist

Rob Hefferan likes to reminisce about the simple life he had as a child growing up in Cheshire, when his biggest worry was whether to have fish fingers or Alphabetti Spaghetti for tea. The faces, colors, and shapes from that time are a present-day inspiration for his artwork.

ISBN-13: 978-0-328-47848-4
ISBN-10:   0-328-47848-2

2 3 4 5 6 7 8 9 10 V042 14 13 12 11 10
CC1

Dear Texas Reader,

Wow! School has started! Did you know that we are about to take a trip along Reading Street? AlphaBuddy and your very own book, *My Skills Buddy,* will be with you for the whole trip.

Let's get ready. Pack your thinking caps. On Reading Street we will be busy learning to read and write and think. It will be hard work, but it will be fun.

You will meet lots of interesting characters. We'll make a stop in Trucktown too.

As AlphaBuddy likes to say, "Let's get this show on the road!"

Sincerely,
The Authors

All Together Now

How do we live, work, and play together?

Big Book

Week 2

Big Book

Realistic Fiction • Social Studies
We Are So Proud! by Donna Longo

Unit 1 Contents

Week 5

Big Book

Week 6

Big Book

Don Leu
The Internet Guy

Right before our eyes, the nature of reading and learning is changing. The Internet and other technologies create new opportunities, new solutions, and new literacies. New reading comprehension skills are required online. They are increasingly important to our students and our society.

Those of us on the Reading Street team are here to help you on this new, and very exciting, journey.

See It!

- **Big Question Video**

- **Concept Talk Video**

- **Envision It! Animations**

- **eReaders**

Hear It!

- *Sing with Me* **Animations**

- **eSelections**

- **Grammar Jammer**

Adam and Kim **play at the beach.**

Concept Talk Video

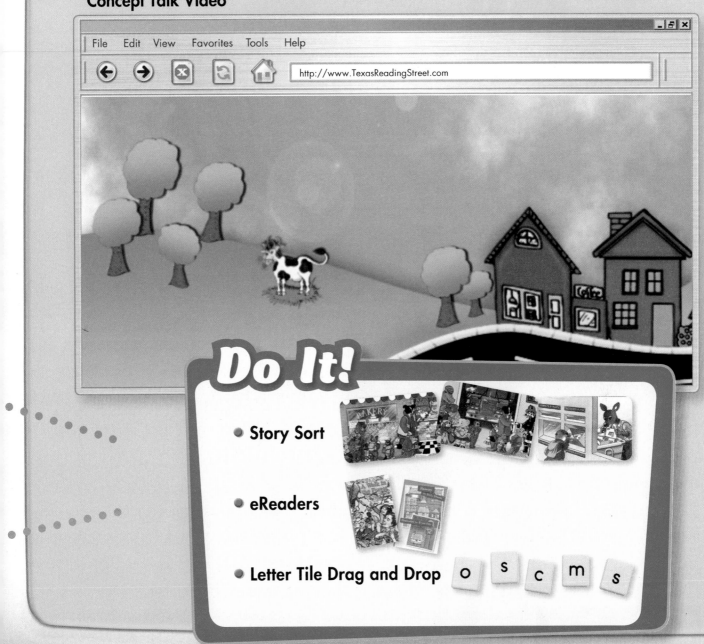

File   Edit   View   Favorites   Tools   Help

http://www.TexasReadingStreet.com

Do It!

- **Story Sort**

- **eReaders**

- **Letter Tile Drag and Drop**   o s c m s

All Together Now

THE BIG
?

How do we live,
work, and play
together?

TEKS

K.2.C.1 Orally generate rhymes in response to spoken words.
K.2.D.1 Distinguish orally presented rhyming pairs of words from non-rhyming pairs.

Phonological Awareness

Let's Listen for

Rhyming Words

Read Together

● Find things that rhyme.

■ What rhymes with *man*? with *mop*? with *coat*? with *book*?

▲ Which word pairs rhyme: *nap/lap, cook/coat, boat/goat*?

READING STREET ONLINE
BIG QUESTION VIDEO
www.TexasReadingStreet.com

TEKS
K.6.A.2 Identify elements of a story including character. **K.8.B** Describe characters in a story and the reasons for their actions.

Comprehension

Envision It!

Literary Elements

READING STREET ONLINE
ENVISION IT! ANIMATIONS
www.TexasReadingStreet.com

Characters

Setting

Plot

15

Envision It! | **Letters to Know**

Aa

Read Together

astronaut

Bb

baby

READING STREET ONLINE
ALPHABET CARDS
www.TexasReadingStreet.com

Print Awareness

Letter Recognition

Letters I Know

A a

B b

16

Words I Can Read

I

am

Sentences I Can Read

1. I am .

2. I am ☺ .

TEKS

K.1.B Identify upper- and lower-case letters. **K.3.D** Identify and read at least 25 high-frequency words from a commonly used list.

Phonics

I Can Read!

Decodable Reader

● Letter Recognition
Aa
Bb
Cc
Dd
Ee

■ High-Frequency Words
I
am

▲ Read the story.

**READING STREET ONLINE
DECODABLE eREADERS**
www.TexasReadingStreet.com

Who Am I?

Written by Bob Atkins
Illustrated by Yvette Pierre

Decodable Reader 1

I am Ann.

I am Ben.

I am Cam.

I am Dot.

I am Ed.

I am Emma.

I am Dad.

TEKS

K.6.A.2 Identify elements of a story including character. **K.8.A.1** Retell a main event from a story read aloud. **RC-K.E.1** Retell important events in stories. **RC-K.F.1** Make connections to own experiences.

Envision It! Retell

Big Book

Think, Talk, and Write

1. How do you get to school? **Text to Self**

2. Which is a character from *The Little School Bus*? **Character**

3. Look back and write.

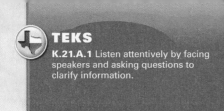

Vocabulary

- Talk about the pictures.
- Which do you use?

Listening and Speaking

- Point to the picture of the bus.
- Cover the picture of the bus with your hand.
- Pretend to drive a bus.

Words for Transportation

bus

car

van

bike

Follow Directions

Be a good listener!

TEKS

K.4.B.2 Respond to questions about texts read aloud. **K.6.A.2** Identify elements of a story including character. **K.6.A.3** Identify elements of a story including key events. **K.8.A.1** Retell a main event from a story read aloud.

King Midas and the Golden Touch

Let's Practice It!

Myth

- Listen to the myth.
- How does it begin?
- Who is King Midas?
- How does King Midas get the "golden touch"?
- What lesson does King Midas learn?

Let's Listen for

Syllables

Read Together

● Point to a picture, say the word, and clap for each part, or syllable, you hear.

■ Which words have one part, or syllable?

▲ Which words have more than one part, or syllable?

READING STREET ONLINE
BIG QUESTION VIDEO
www.TexasReadingStreet.com

32

TEKS
K.6.A.1 Identify elements of a story including setting.

Comprehension

Envision It!

Literary Elements

READING STREET ONLINE
ENVISION IT! ANIMATIONS
www.TexasReadingStreet.com

Characters

Setting

34

Plot

TEKS
K.1.A.1 Recognize that spoken words can be represented by print. **K.1.C.1** Demonstrate the one-to-one correspondence between a spoken and a printed word. **K.1.D.1** Recognize the difference between a letter and a printed word. **Also K.1.B, K.1.E.1.**

Envision It! | Letters to Know

Read Together

Cc
cactus

Dd
dolphin

Ee
escalator

Ff
fountain

Gg
goose

Hh
helicopter

Ii
igloo

Print Awareness

Letter Recognition

Letters I Know

Cc Dd Ee

Ff Gg Hh

Ii

cab

The cab is yellow.

Words I Can Read

I

am

Sentences I Can Read

1. I am .

2. Am I ?

TEKS

K.1.B Identify upper- and lower-case letters. **K.3.D** Identify and read at least 25 high-frequency words from a commonly used list.

Phonics

I Can Read!

Decodable Reader

● Letter Recognition
Ff
Gg
Hh
Ii
Jj
Kk
Ll

■ High-Frequency Words
I
am

▲ Read the story.

Am I?

Written by George Helm
Illustrated by Tori Wheaton

Decodable Reader 2

I am Jan.

Am I Fran?

I am Len.

Am I Ken?

I am Kim.

Am I Hanna?

I am Gus.

Envision It! Retell

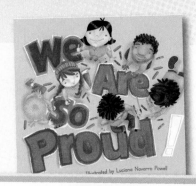

Big Book

Think, Talk, and Write

Read Together

1. How do we work and play together? Text to Self

2. Where does the story *We Are So Proud!* take place?

Setting

3. Look back and write.

TEKS

K.5.C Identify and sort pictures of objects into conceptual categories.
K.23.A.2 Follow agreed-upon rules for discussion, including speaking one at a time.

Vocabulary

● What do you see that is red?

■ What do you see that is white?

▲ What do you see that is blue?

Listening and Speaking

● Where does the story take place?

■ What is your favorite part of the story? Why?

▲ Who is your favorite character in the story? Why?

Vocabulary

Color Words

red

white

blue

48

Respond to Literature
Drama

Carol Roth
The Little School Bus

Illustrated by
Pamela Paparone

Be a good speaker!

TEKS

K.9.A.1 Identify the topic of an informational text heard. **K.10.A** Identify the topic and details in expository text heard or read, referring to the words and/or illustrations. **K.10.B.1** Retell important facts in a text, heard or read.

The United States Flag

Let's Practice It!

Expository Text

● Listen to the selection.

■ What is this selection about?

▲ How are the two flags alike? How are they different?

★ Why does the U.S. flag have 13 stripes?

♥ What do the 50 stars on the U.S. flag stand for?

U.S. Flag Today

First U.S. Flag

TEKS

K.2.E.1 Recognize spoken alliteration or groups of words that begin with the same spoken onset or initial sound. **K.2.H.1** Isolate the initial sound in one-syllable spoken words.

Phonemic Awareness

Let's Listen for

Read Together

Initial Sounds

● Point to something that begins like *pig*. Say the word. Say the beginning sound.

■ Find other things in the picture that begin like *pig*. Say the words.

▲ Say these words: *pie, pumpkin, pepper.* Do they begin the same? What about *pears, cakes, apples?*

READING STREET ONLINE
BIG QUESTION VIDEO
www.TexasReadingStreet.com

53

Comprehension

Envision It!

Sequence

READING STREET ONLINE
ENVISION IT! ANIMATIONS
www.TexasReadingStreet.com

TEKS

K.1.A.1 Recognize that spoken words can be represented by print. **K.1.C.1** Demonstrate the one-to-one correspondence between a spoken and a printed word. **K.1.D.1** Recognize the difference between a letter and a word. **Also K.1.B, K.1.E.1.**

Envision It! | Letters to Know

Read Together

Jj — jaguar

Kk — koala

Ll — lemon

Mm — motorcycle

Nn — nest

Oo — otter

Pp — penguin

READING STREET ONLINE
ALPHABET CARDS
www.TexasReadingStreet.com

Print Awareness

Letter Recognition

Letters I Know

Jj Kk Ll

Mm Nn

Oo Pp

mop

The mop is wet.

Words I Can Read

the

little

Sentences I Can Read

1. I am little.

2. I am the little .

TEKS

K.1.B Identify upper- and lower-case letters. **K.3.D** Identify and read at least 25 high-frequency words from a commonly used list.

Phonics

I Can
Read!

Decodable Reader

- Letter Recognition
  Mm
  Nn
  Oo
  Pp
  Qq
  Rr
  Ss

- High-Frequency Words
  I
  am
  the
  little

▲ Read the story.

Decodable Reader 3

The Little Toys

Written by Roger Jons
Illustrated by Scott Salinski

 I am the little robot.

I am the little puzzle.

I am the little queen.

I am the little octopus.

I am the little train.

I am the little block.

I am the little spaceship.

TEKS

K.8.A.1 Retell a main event from a story read aloud. ★ Describe the events of a story in order.

Envision It! Retell

Big Book

Think, Talk, and Write

1. How do you help your family? _{Text to Self}

2. What happens first in the story? What happens last?

Sequence

3. Look back and write.

TEKS

K.21.A.1 Listen attentively by facing speakers. **K.5.C** Identify and sort pictures of objects into conceptual categories.

Let's Learn It!

Vocabulary

- ● Look around for squares and circles.
- ■ Look around for triangles and rectangles.
- ▲ Which shape is your favorite?

Listening and Speaking

- ● Name the words that rhyme.

Words for Shapes

square

circle

triangle

rectangle

Listen for Rhyme and Rhythm

Be a good listener!

The Boy Who Cried Wolf!

Let's Practice It!

Fable

● Listen to the fable.

■ Why does the shepherd boy cry "Wolf!" the first two times?

▲ What lesson does the shepherd boy learn? Has anything like this ever happened to you? Tell about it.

★ What do you think the shepherd boy might do next?

♥ A moral is a type of expression. What new expression does this fable teach you?

TEKS
K.2.E.1 Recognize spoken alliteration or groups of words that begin with the same spoken onset or initial sound. **K.2.H.1** Isolate the initial sound in spoken one-syllable words.

Phonemic Awareness

Let's Listen for

Initial Sounds

Read Together

● Point to the pig in the puddle. Say "a pig in a puddle." What sound do you hear repeated?

■ Point to the man with the mouse. Say "a man with a mouse." What sound is repeated?

▲ Find things that begin with /b/, /d/, /k/, /p/, and /m/.

★ Name two things that begin like *ball*, *desk*, *key*, *pen*, and *met*.

READING STREET ONLINE
BIG QUESTION VIDEO
www.TexasReadingStreet.com

Comprehension

Envision It!

Classify and Categorize

READING STREET ONLINE
ENVISION IT! ANIMATIONS
www.TexasReadingStreet.com

TEKS

K.1.E Recognize that sentences are comprised of words separated by spaces and demonstrate the awareness of word boundaries. **K.2.A.1** Identify a sentence made up of a group of words. **Also K.1.B, K.1.C.1, K.1.D.1.**

Envision It! | **Letters to Know**

Qq
queen

Rr
river

Ss
salamander

Tt
turtle

Uu
umbrella

Vv
volcano

Read Together

Print Awareness

Letter Recognition

Letters I Know

Q q   R r   S s

T t   U u   V v

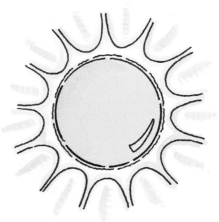

sun

The sun is hot.

Words I Can Read

the

little

Sentences I Can Read

1. Am I little?

2. I am the little .

TEKS
K.1.B Identify upper- and lower-case letters. **K.3.D** Identify and read at least 25 high-frequency words from a commonly used list.

Phonics

I Can Read!

Decodable Reader

● Letter Recognition
Tt
Uu
Vv
Ww
Xx
Yy
Zz

■ High-Frequency Words
I
am
the
little

▲ Read the story.

READING STREET ONLINE
DECODABLE eREADERS
www.TexasReadingStreet.com

At the Zoo

Written by Nitty Jones

Illustrated by Amy Sparks

Decodable Reader 4

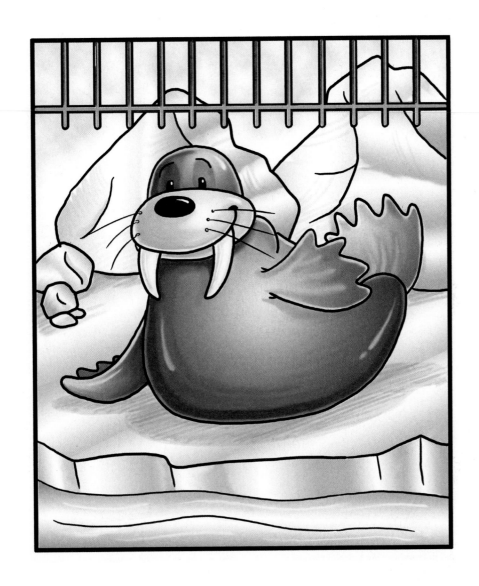

I am the little walrus.

 I am the little tiger.

I am the little yak.

I am the little ox.

I am the little rhino.

I am the little zebra.

I am the little umbrella bird.

TEKS

K.5.C Identify and sort pictures of objects into conceptual categories. **K.8.A.1** Retell a main event from a story read aloud. **RC-K.E.1** Retell important events in stories. **RC-K.F.3** Make connections to the larger community.

Envision It! Retell

Big Book

Think, Talk, and Write

1. Who helps in our town?

Text to World

2. Which things belong together?

Classify and Categorize

3. Look back and write.

TEKS

K.5.A Identify and use words that name locations. **K.22** Share information by speaking audibly and clearly using the conventions of language. **K.23.A.2** Follow agreed-upon rules for discussion, including speaking one at a time.

Let's Learn It!

Vocabulary

● Talk about the pictures.

■ Where do you go in your neighborhood?

Listening and Speaking

▲ What is your favorite color? Why do you like it?

Vocabulary

Location Words

library

park

school

post office

Tell About Me

Be a good speaker!

TEKS
K.4.B.2 Respond to questions about texts read aloud. **K.5.A.1** Identify words that name actions. **K.11.A.1** Follow pictorial directions. **RC-K.A.2** Discuss the purposes for listening to various texts.

Curry Veggie Dip

Step 1

Let's Practice It!

Recipe

- ● Listen to the recipe.
- ■ What is the third step in the recipe?
- ▲ Which words in the recipe name actions for you to do?
- ★ Why do people read recipes?

Step 2

Step 3

Step 4

TEKS
K.2.E.1 Recognize spoken alliteration or groups of words that begin with the same spoken onset or initial sound.
K.2.H.1 Isolate the initial sound in spoken one-syllable words.

Let's Listen for

Initial Sounds

Read Together

● Point to the man in the ticket booth. Say "Man makes money." What sound do you hear at the beginning of those words?

▲ Find three things in the picture that begin with /m/.

★ Name other words that begin with /m/.

READING STREET ONLINE
BIG QUESTION VIDEO
www.TexasReadingStreet.com

TEKS

K.6.A.2 Identify elements of a story including character. **K.8.B** Describe characters in a story and the reasons for their actions.

Comprehension

Envision It!

Literary Elements

READING STREET ONLINE
ENVISION IT! ANIMATION
www.TexasReadingStreet.com

Characters

Setting

Plot

TEKS

K.1.D.1 Recognize the difference between a letter and a printed word. **K.1.E** Recognize that sentences are comprised of words separated by spaces and demonstrate the awareness of word boundaries. **Also K.1.B, K.1.C.1.**

Envision It! | Letters to Know

Read Together

Ww

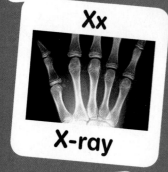

watermelon

Xx

X-ray

Yy

yo-yo

Zz

zigzag

Print Awareness

Letter Recognition

Letters I Know

W w X x

Y y Z z

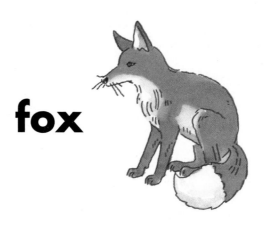

fox

The fox is red.

Words I Can Read

to

a

Sentences I Can Read

1. I am a  .

2. I to a .

TEKS

K.1.B Identify upper- and lower-case letters. K.3.A.1 Identify the common sounds that letters represent. K.3.D Identify and read at least 25 high-frequency words from a commonly used list.

Phonics

I Can Read!

Decodable Reader

- Consonant Mm (with rebus)
  monkey
  mule
  mouse
  minnow
  moth
  mole
  moose

- High-Frequency Words
  I
  am
  a
  little

▲ Read the story.

**READING STREET ONLINE
DECODABLE eREADERS**
www.TexasReadingStreet.com

Decodable Reader 5

Animal Friends

Written by Phil Morton
Illustrated by Julie Word

I am a little monkey.

I am a little mule.

I am a little mouse.

 I am a little minnow.

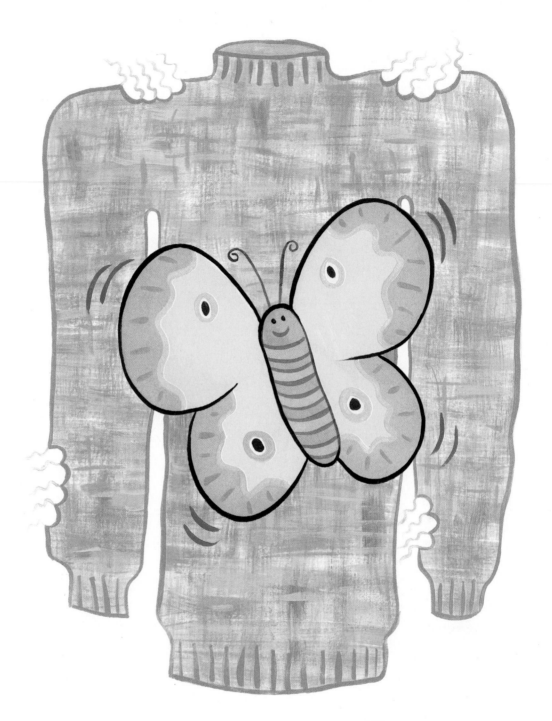

I am a little moth.

I am a little mole.

I am a little moose.
Am I little?

TEKS

K.6.A.2 Identify elements of a story including character. **K.8.A.1** Retell a main event from a story read aloud. **K.8.B.1** Describe characters in a story. **RC-K.E.1** Retell important events in stories. **RC-K.F.1** Make connections to own experiences.

Envision It! | Retell

Big Book

READING STREET ONLINE
STORY SORT
www.TexasReadingStreet.com

Think, Talk, and Write

1. What do you do with your friends? **Text to Self**

2. Which is a character from *Smash! Crash!*? **Character**

3. Look back and write.

TEKS

K.5.A Identify and use words that name positions. **K.23.A.2** Follow agreed-upon rules for discussion, including taking turns and speaking one at a time.

Let's Learn It!

Vocabulary

- ● Talk about the pictures.

- ■ Put your hand up . . . now down.

- ▲ Put your hand in your pocket. Now take it out.

Listening and Speaking

- ● Make an announcement.

- ■ Listen to a classmate's message or announcement.

- ▲ Retell or summarize your classmate's message or announcement.

Vocabulary

Position Words

in

out

up

down

Announcements/Messages

Be a good speaker!

TEKS

K.9.A.1 Identify the topic of an informational text heard. **K.11.B.2** Identify the meaning of specific signs. **RC-K.A** Discuss purposes for reading and listening to various texts.

At a **Farmer's Market**

Let's **Practice** It!

Signs

● Listen to the selection.

■ What is the selection about?

▲ Point to each sign. Tell what it means.

★ Why does each stand at the market have a sign? Who will read the signs?

♥ How do the signs help Sandra with her plans?

Apples 🍎
10 for $ 1

Farmer's market

TEKS

K.2.E.1 Recognize spoken alliteration or groups of words that begin with the same spoken onset or initial sound. **K.2.H.1** Isolate the initial sound in spoken one-syllable words.

Phonemic Awareness

Let's Listen for

Initial Sounds

Read Together

● Point to the table. Say, "two tan tables." What sound do you hear at the beginning of those words?

▲ Find three things in the picture that begin with /t/.

★ Name other words that begin with /t/.

READING STREET ONLINE
BIG QUESTION VIDEO
www.TexasReadingStreet.com

Comprehension

Envision It!

Classify and Categorize

READING STREET ONLINE
ENVISION IT! ANIMATIONS
www.TexasReadingStreet.com

TEKS
K.1.B Identify upper- and lower-case letters. **K.2.H.1** Isolate the initial sound in spoken words. **K.3.A.1** Identify the common sounds that letters represent. **K.3.D** Identify and read at least 25 high-frequency words from a commonly used list.

Envision It! | Sounds to Know

Read Together

Mm

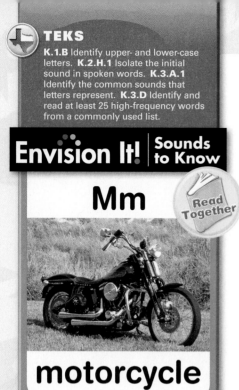

motorcycle

Tt

turtle

READING STREET ONLINE
ALPHABET CARDS
www.TexasReadingStreet.com

Phonics

Initial *m*, Initial *t*

Letter Sounds I Know

M m   M m

T t   T t

Words I Can Read

to

a

Sentences I Can Read

1. I am a little .

2. I 🏃 to 🏫 .

TEKS

K.1.B Identify upper- and lower-case letters. **K.3.A.1** Identify the common sounds that letters represent. **K.3.D** Identify and read at least 25 high-frequency words from a commonly used list.

Phonics

I Can Read!

Decodable Reader

● Consonant Tt
  (with rebus)
  tiger
  turtle
  turkey
  toad
  toucan
  tadpole

■ High-Frequency Words
  I
  to
  a

▲ Read the story.

**READING STREET ONLINE
DECODABLE eREADERS
www.TexasReadingStreet.com**

**Decodable
Reader
6**

Let's Go

Written by Liz Cristie
Illustrated by Larry Jordon

I walk to a tiger.

I walk to a turtle.

 I walk to a turkey.

I walk to a toad.

I walk to a toucan.

I walk to a tadpole.

 I walk home.

TEKS

K.5.C Identify and sort pictures of objects into conceptual categories. **K.10.B** Retell important facts from a text, heard or read. **RC-K.F2** Make connections to ideas in other texts.

Envision It! | Retell

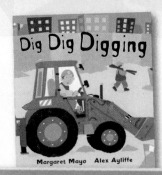

Big Book

Think, Talk, and Write

1. How are the trucks in *Smash! Crash!* and *Dig, Dig, Digging* different?

Text to Text

2. Which things belong together? Classify and Categorize

3. Look back and write.

127

Let's Learn It!

Vocabulary

- Talk about the pictures.
- What do you see that is big? What is little?
- ▲ Who is tall and who is short?

Listening and Speaking

- Where do AlphaBuddy's stories take place?

Vocabulary

Words for Sizes

big

little

tall

short

128

Respond to Literature
Drama

Be a good listener!

TEKS

K.6.B.1 Discuss the big idea of a well-known folk tale. **K.6.B.3** Connect the big idea of a well-known folk tale to personal experience. **K.6.D.3** Recognize recurring phrases in traditional folk tales from various cultures.

Let's Practice It!

Folk Tale

● Listen to the folk tale.

■ What can you tell about the third little pig?

▲ What does the wolf say each time he comes to a house?

★ What lesson do the first two pigs learn?

♥ Why do people like to read or listen to this story?

The Three Little Pigs

1

2

Words for Things That Go

airplane

bike

truck

car

bus

van

boat

train

Words for Colors

white

purple

brown

green

black

pink

blue

red

yellow

orange

Words for Shapes

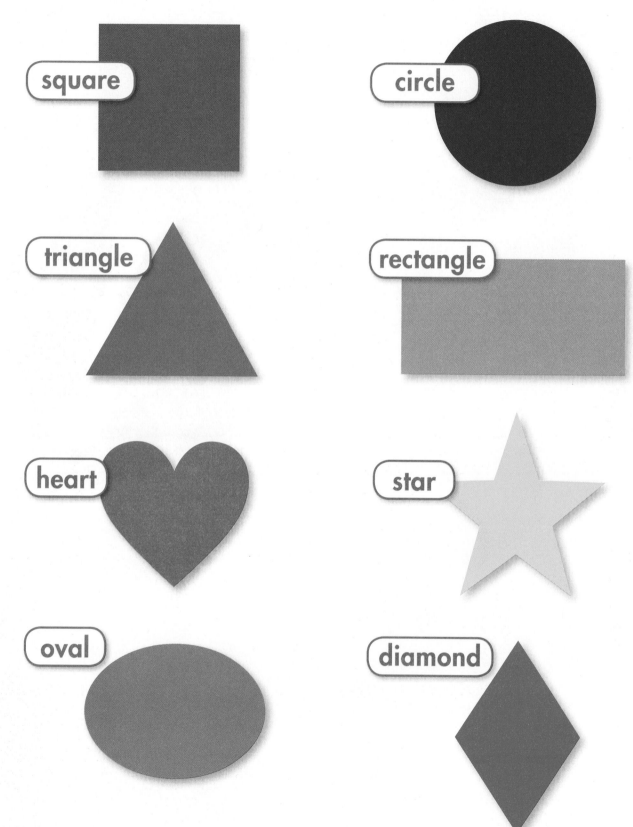

square

circle

triangle

rectangle

heart

star

oval

diamond

Words for Places

school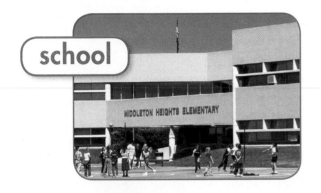

home

park

train station

police station

fire station

post office

library

Words for Animals

lion

mouse

puppy

dog

cat

duck

turtle

kitten

chick

hen

rooster

bird

136

butterfly

fish

whale

caterpillar

bear

panda

beaver

calf

cow

Words for Actions

skip

walk

run

fly

swim

ride

jump

hop

Position Words

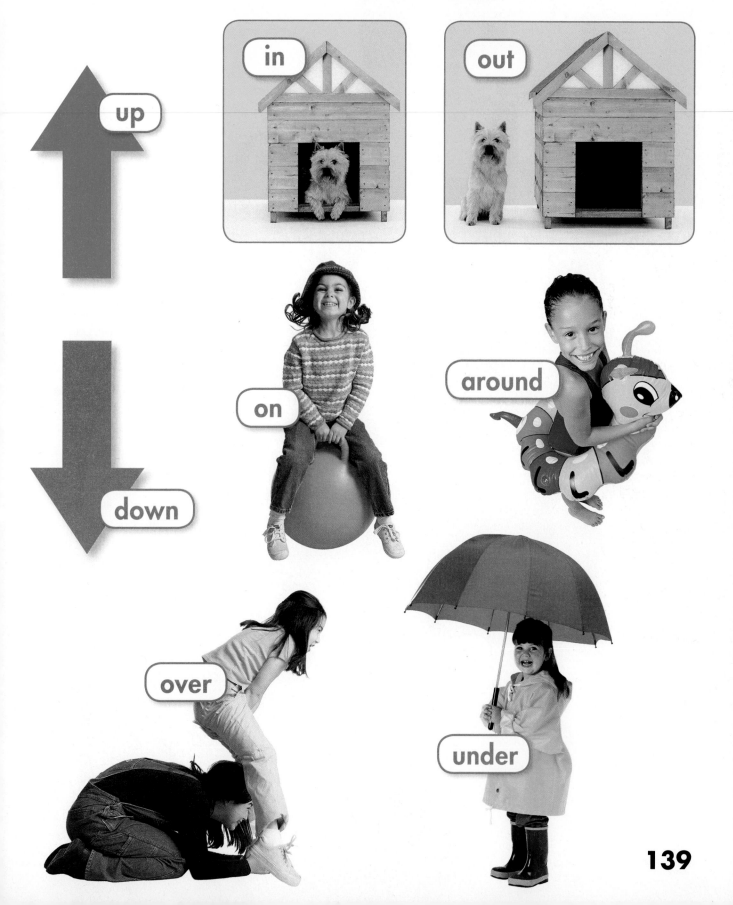

up

down

in

out

on

around

over

under

My Classroom

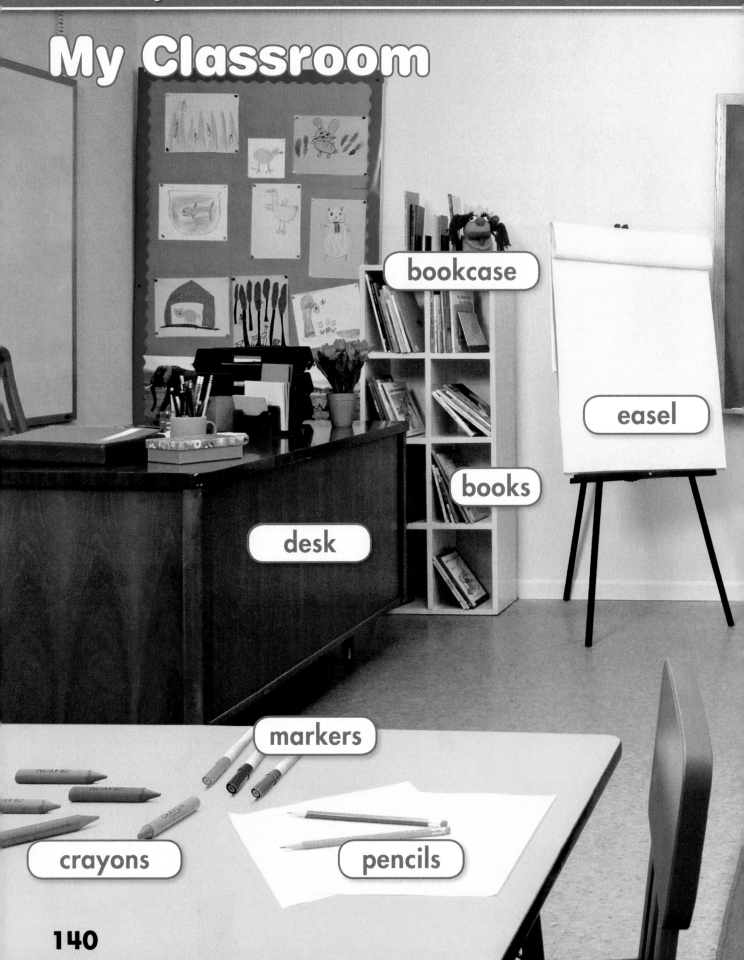

bookcase

easel

books

desk

markers

crayons

pencils

teacher

toys

paper

chair

blocks

table

rug

Words for Feelings

happy

frightened

worried

excited

angry

proud

sad

surprised

My Family

mom
mother

dad
father

sister

grandmother

grandfather

brother

Acknowledgments

Illustrations

Cover: Rob Hefferan

12 Manja Stojic

19–25, 300 Maria Mola

30–31 C. B. Canga

32 Stephen Lewis

39–45, 300 Cale Atkinson

48, 89, 108–110 Mick Reid

52 Ariel Pang

59–65, 300 Natalia Vasquez

70–71 Akemi Gutierrez

72 Amanda Haley

79–85, 300 Robbie Short

92 Ken Wilson Max

112 Jamie Smith

119–125, 300 Dani Jones

130–131 John Ashton Golden

300 Wednesday Kirwan.

The *Texas Essential Knowledge and Skills for English Language Arts and Reading* reproduced by permission, Texas Education Agency, 1701 N. Congress Avenue, Austin, TX 78701

Photographs

Every effort has been made to secure permission and provide appropriate credit for photographic material. The publisher deeply regrets any omission and pledges to correct errors called to its attention in subsequent editions.

Unless otherwise acknowledged, all photographs are the property of Pearson Education, Inc.

Photo locators denoted as follows: Top (T), Center (C), Bottom (B), Left (L), Right (R), Background (Bkgd)

10 (B) ©Michael Keller/Corbis

28 ©Drive Images/Alamy Images, ©Lew Robertson/Corbis, ©Motoring Picture Library/Alamy Images, Getty Images

29 ©Alan Schein Photography/Corbis, ©Ron Chapple/Corbis

87 (T, C) Jupiter Images

88 ©Andersen Ross/Blend Images/Corbis, ©Derrick Alderman/Alamy Images, ©Ellen Isaacs/Alamy Images, ©Corbis/Jupiter Images

109 ©Jim Craigmyle/Corbis, ©Peter Christopher/Masterfile Corporation

127 (C) ©DK Images, (T) Getty Images

128 ©Corbis/Jupiter Images, Jupiter Images

129 ©ImageState/Alamy Images, ©Ron Buskirk/Alamy Images, Jupiter Images

133 (B) Getty Images.